BUTTERFLIES AND FLOWERS

COLORING BOOK FOR KIDS

THIS BOOK BELONGS TO

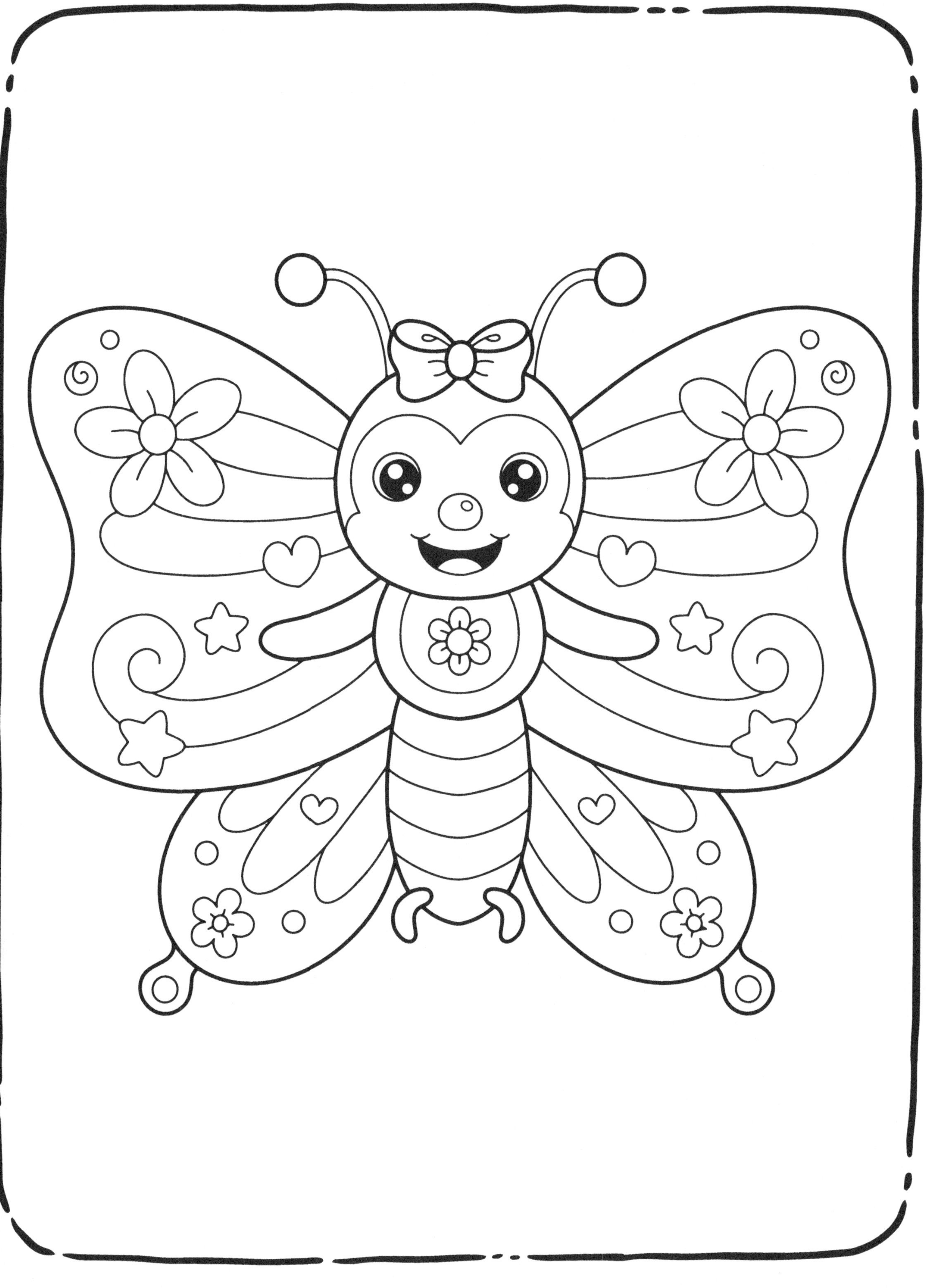

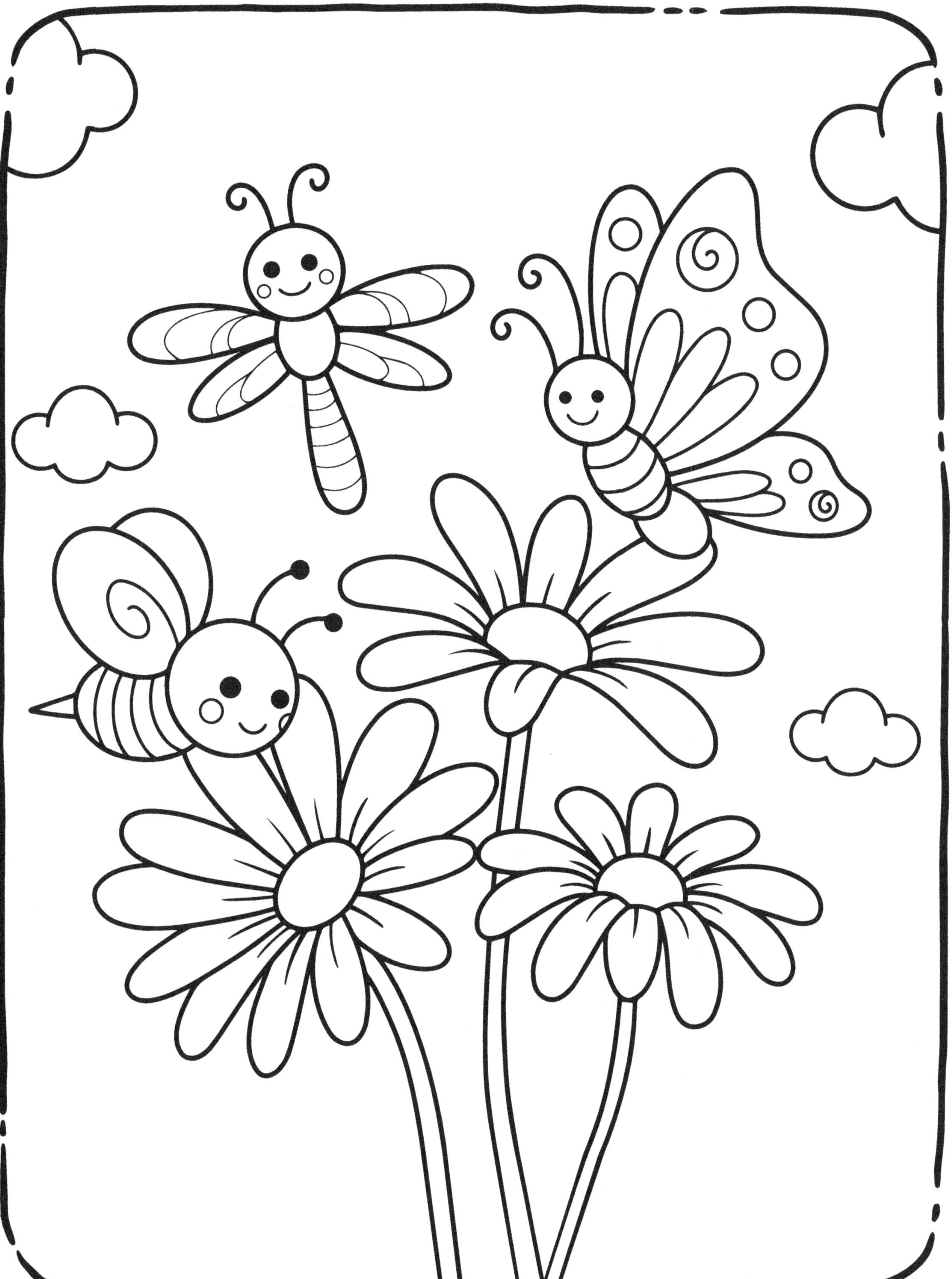

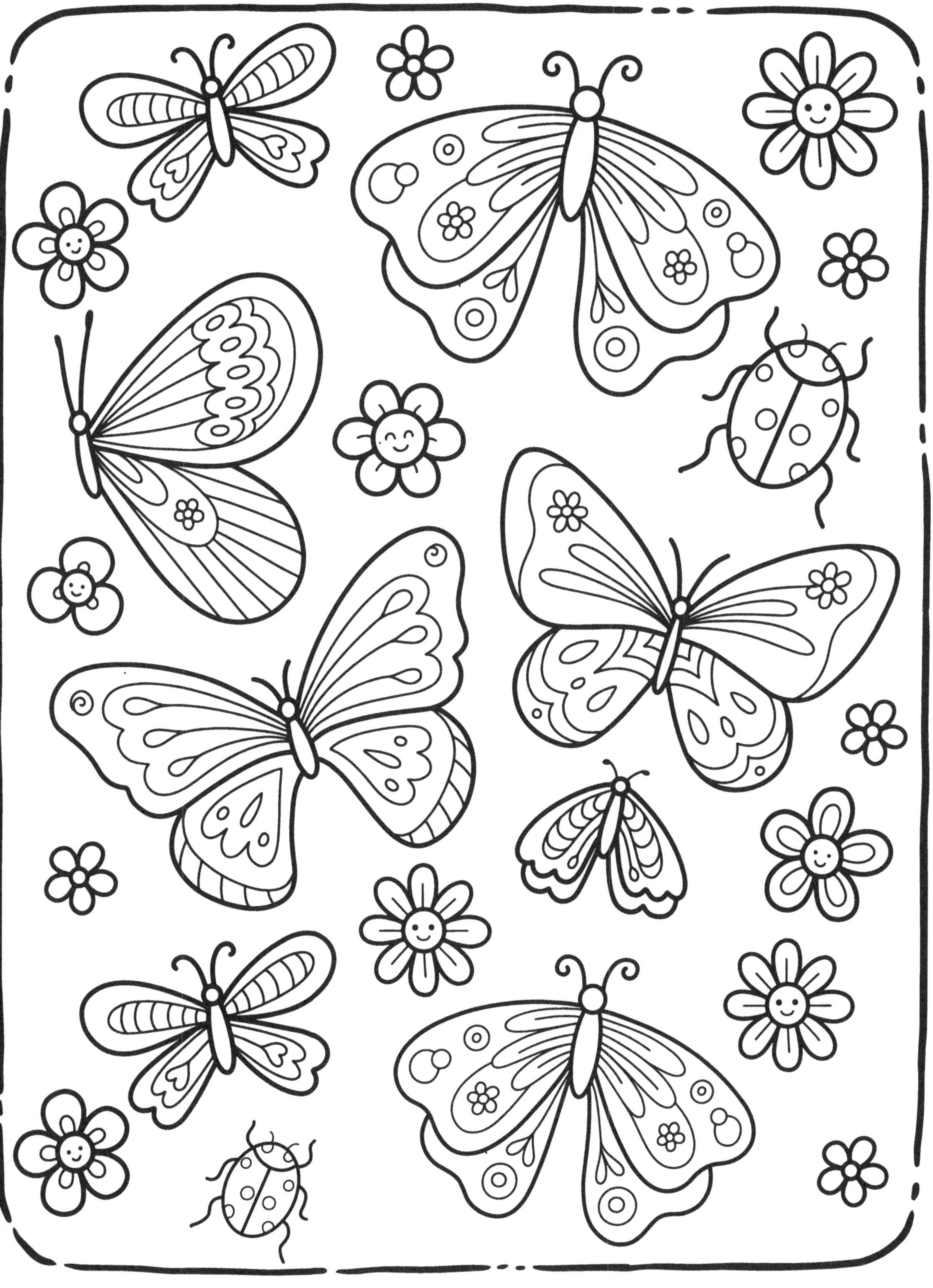

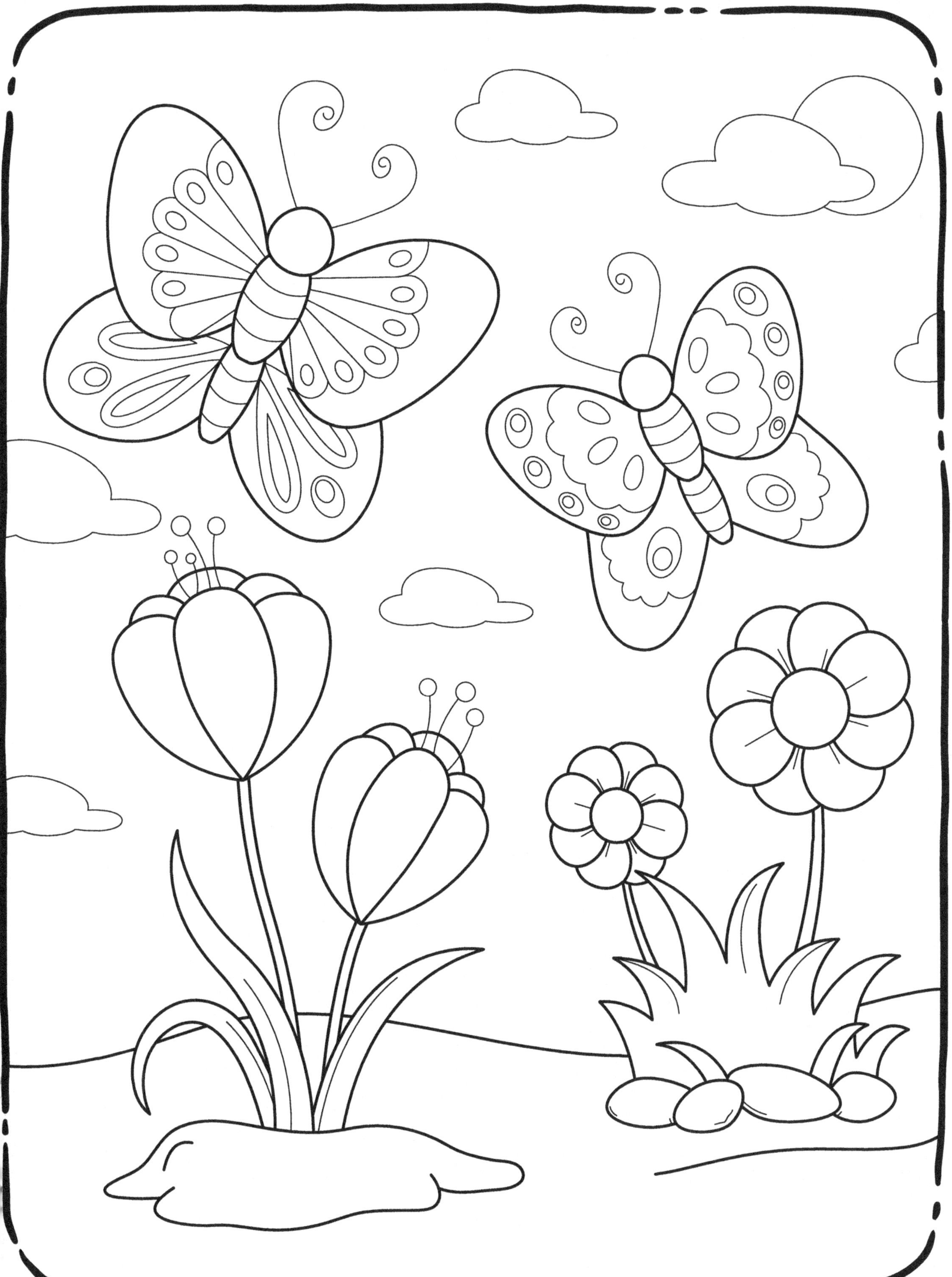

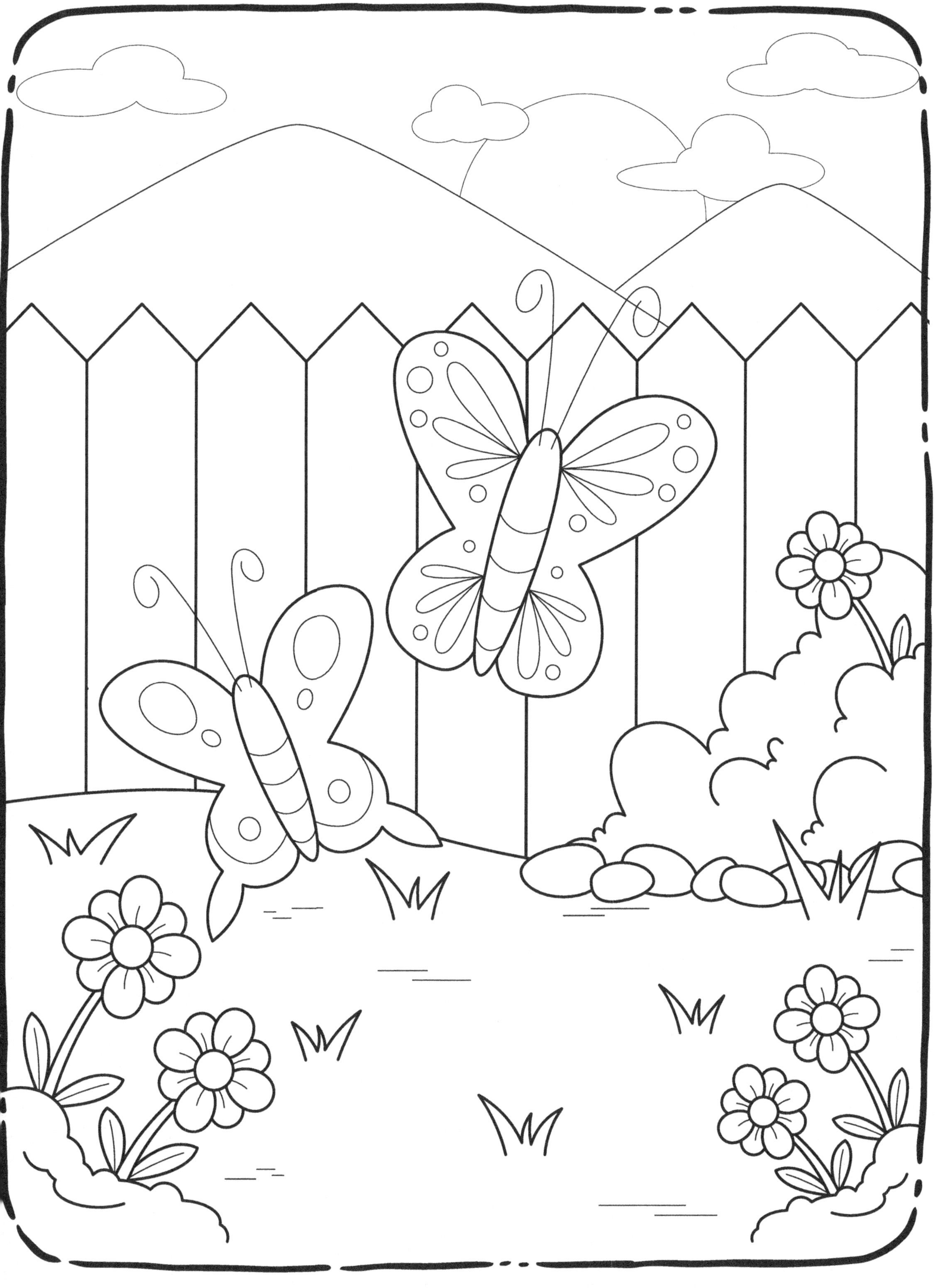

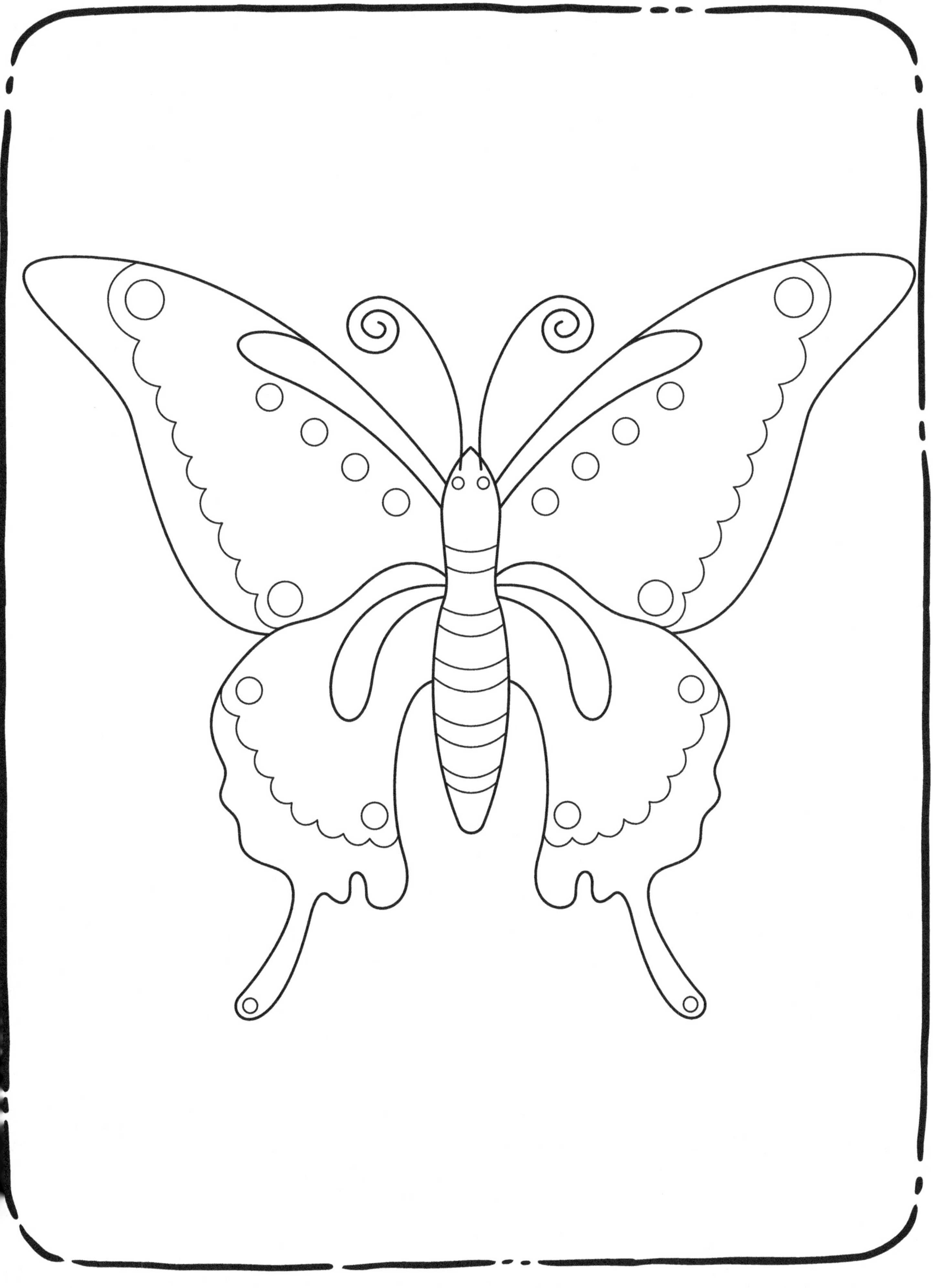

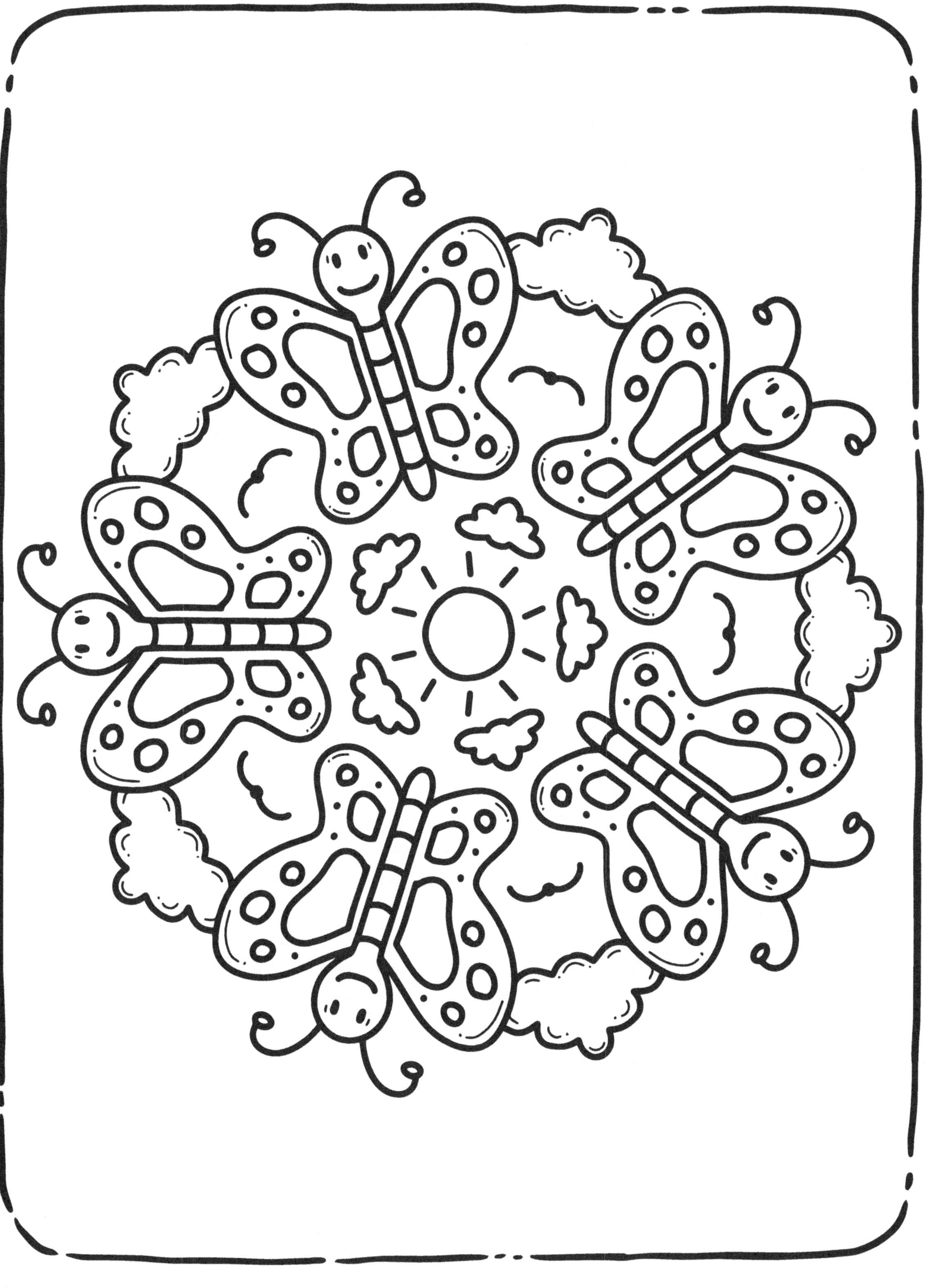

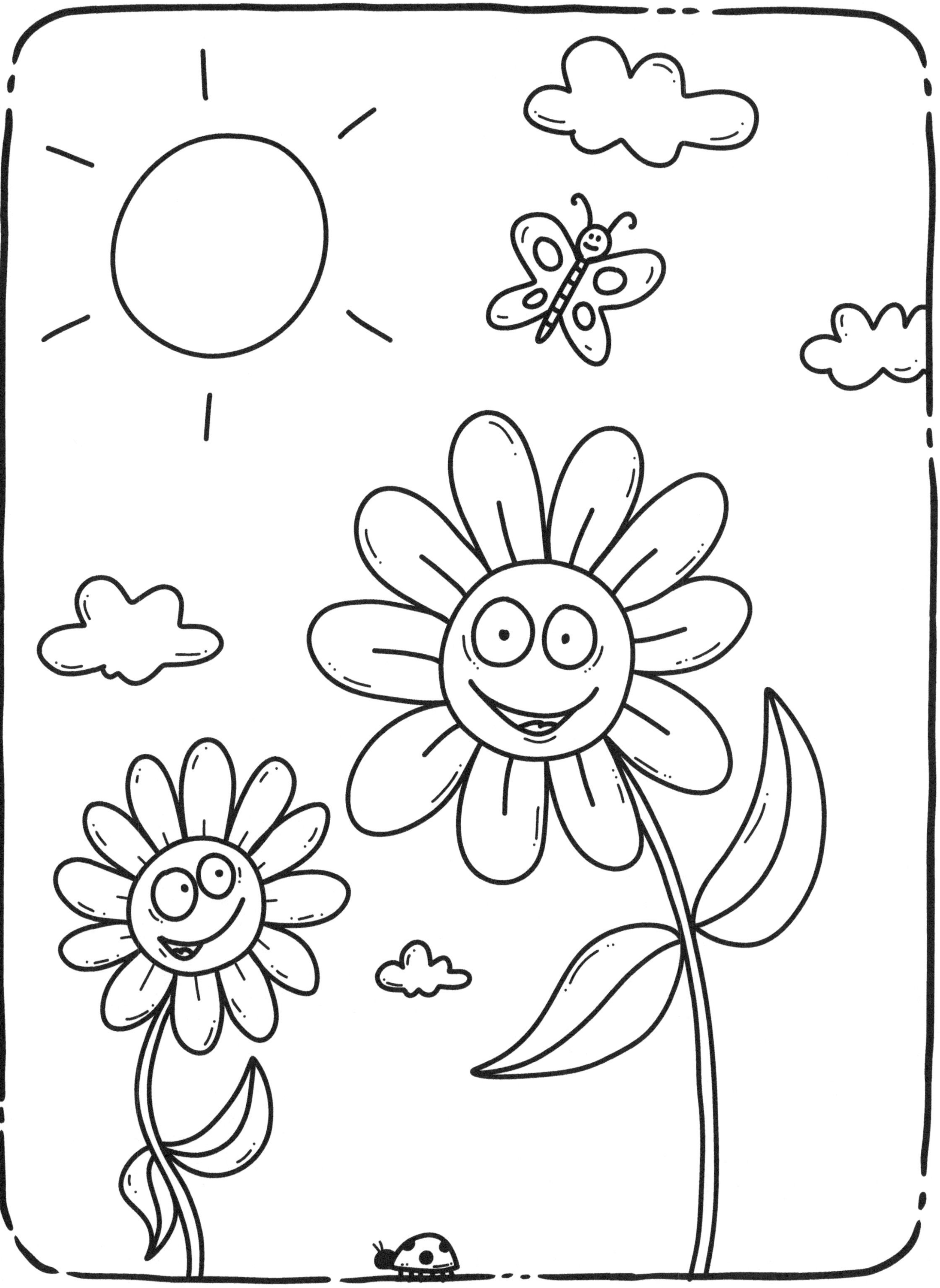

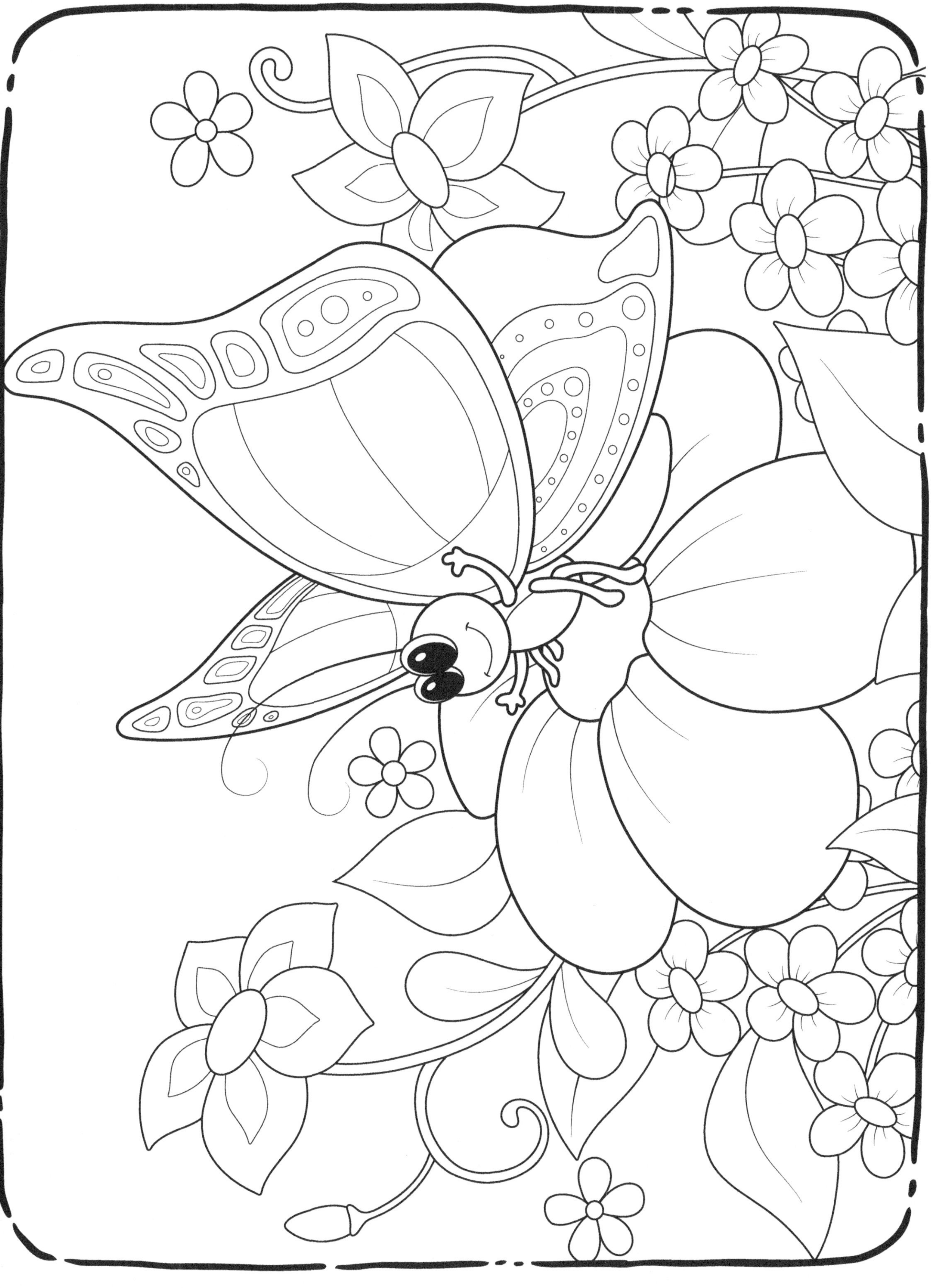

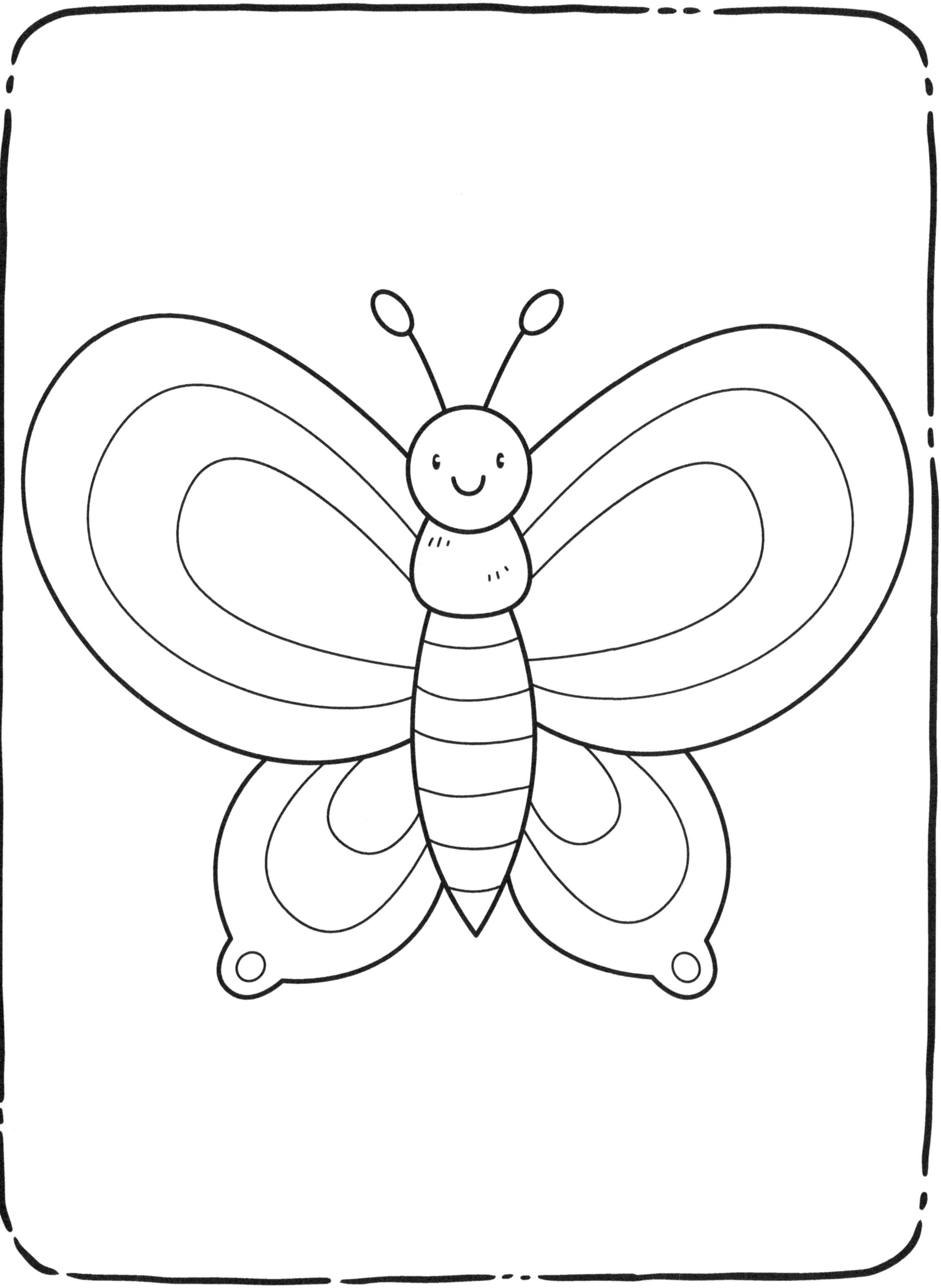

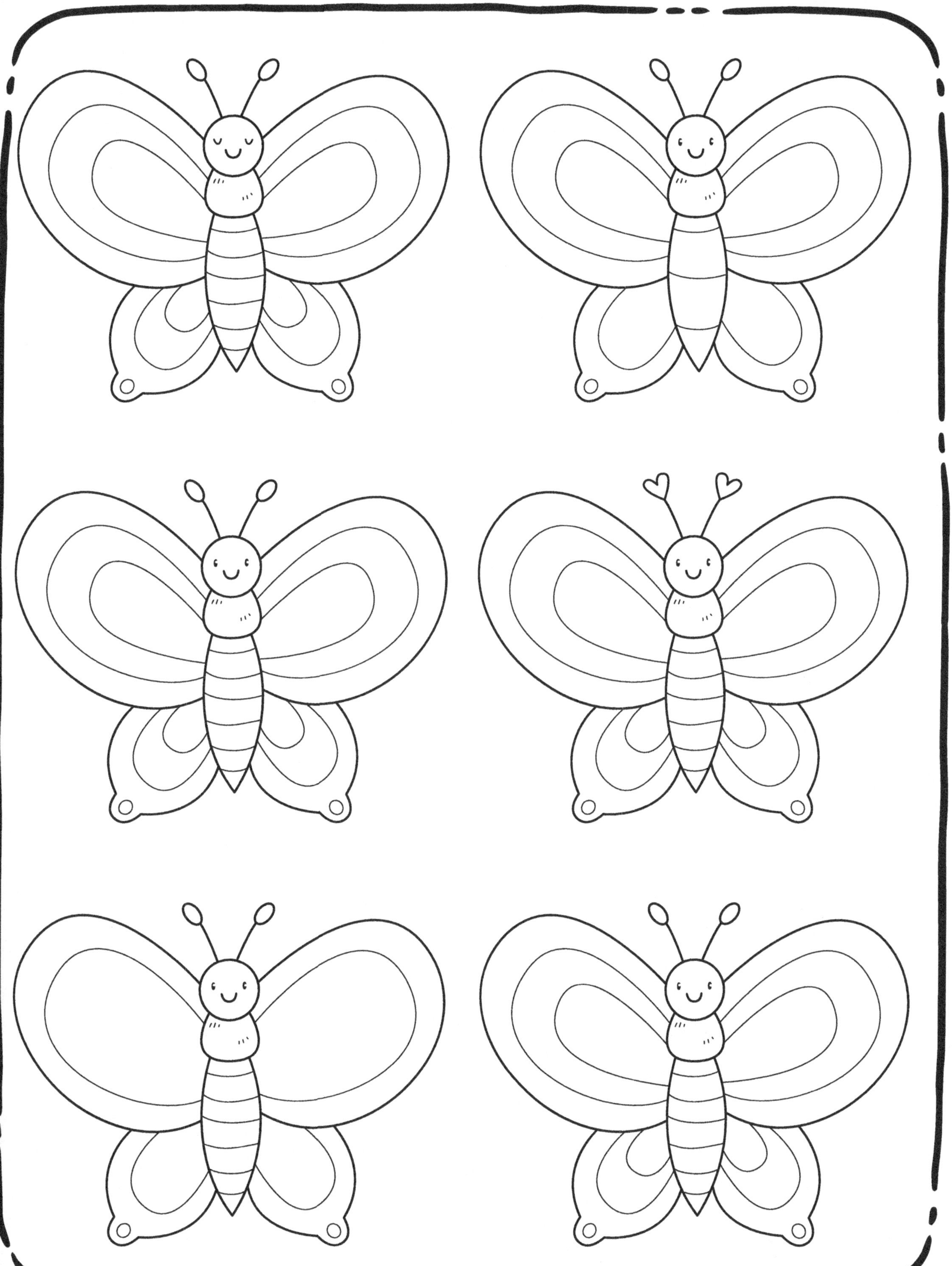

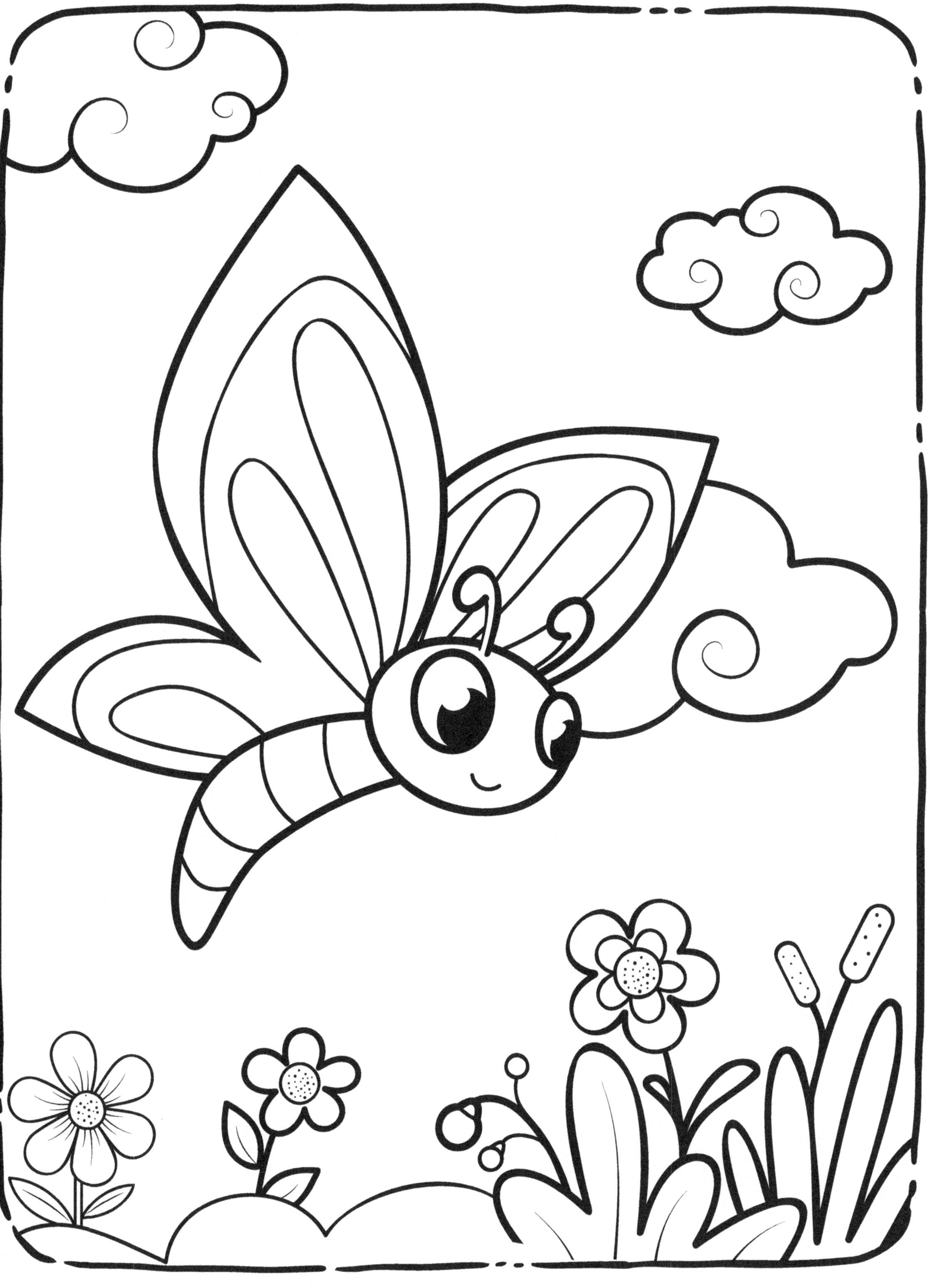

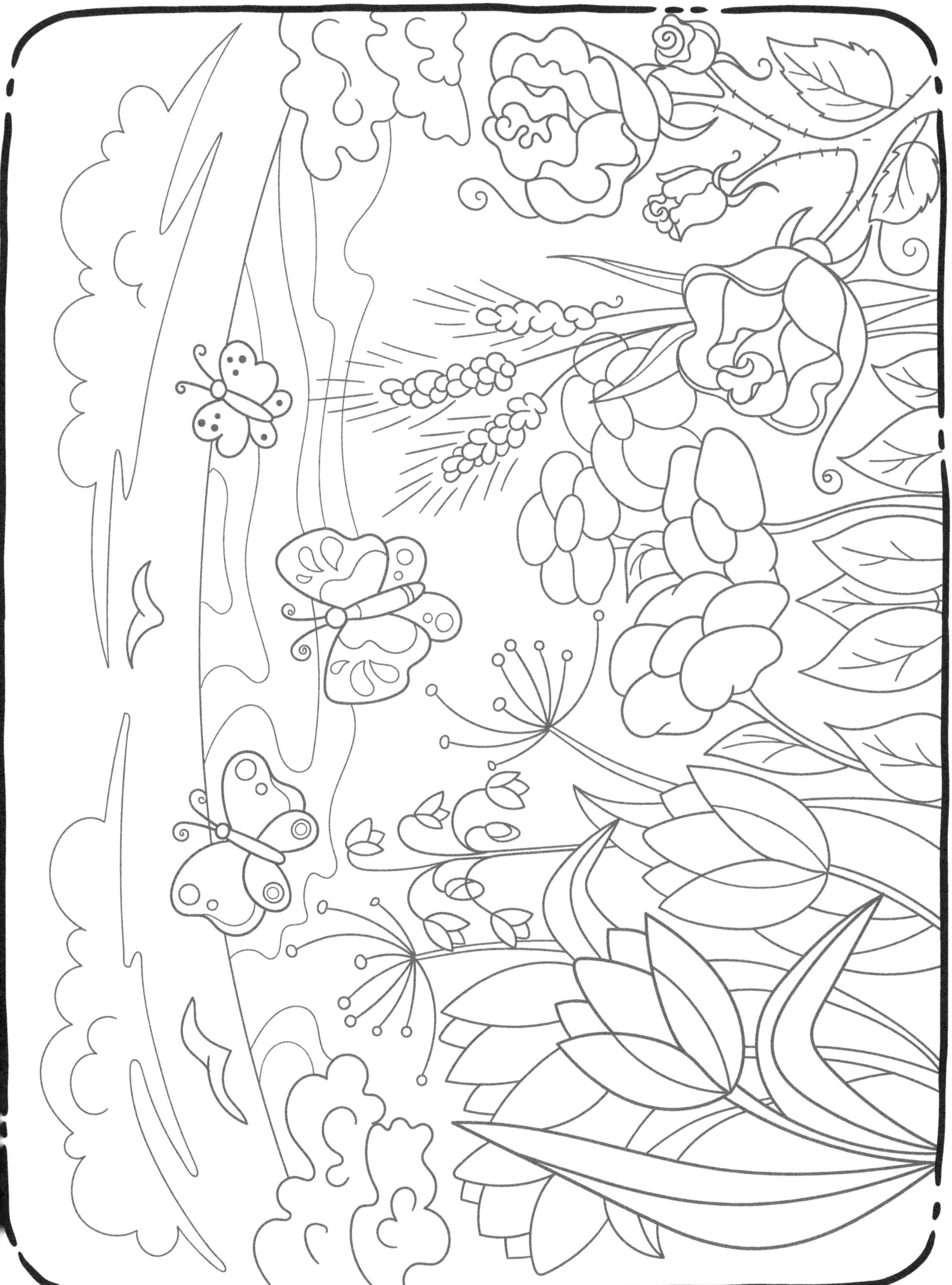

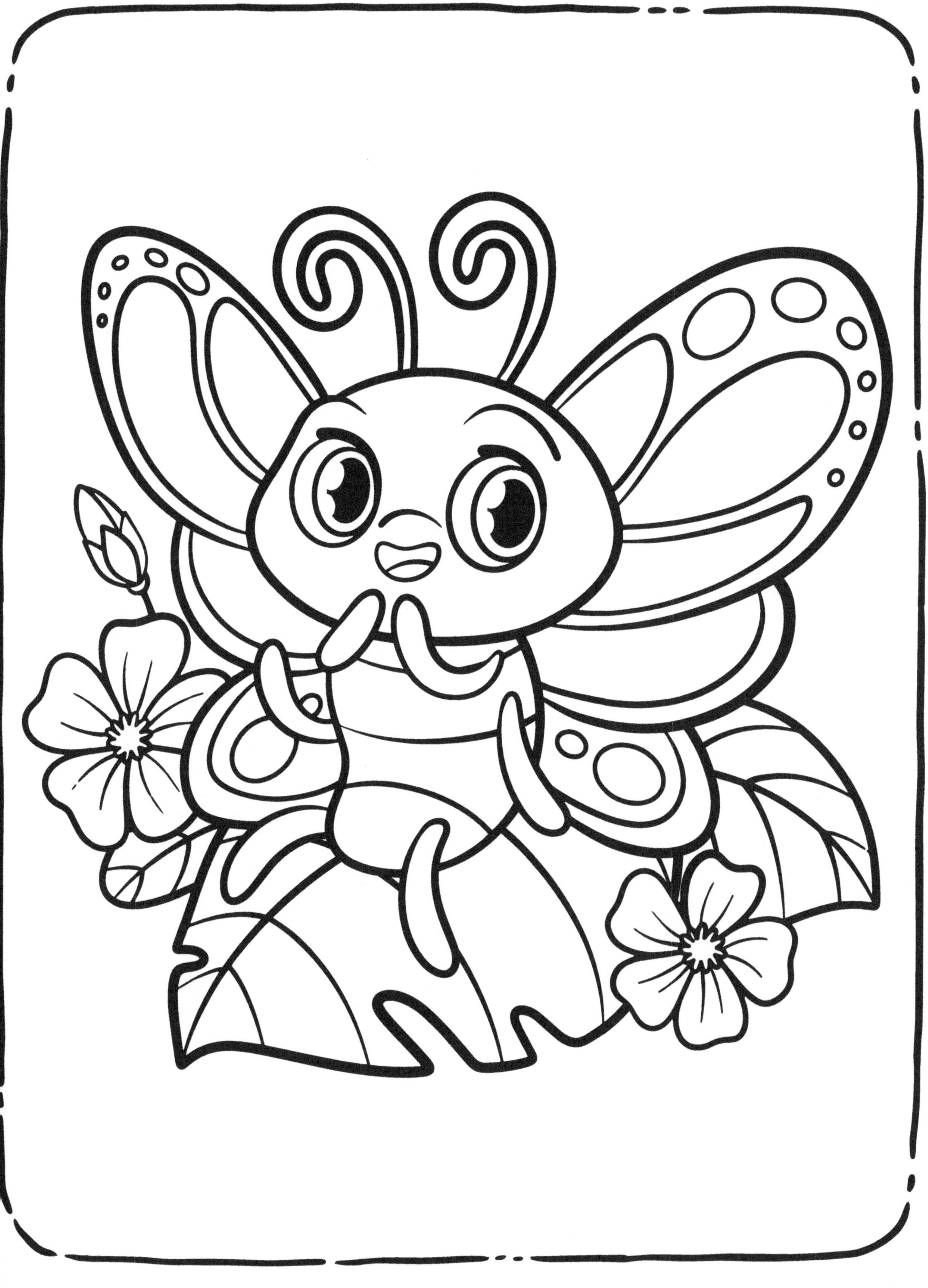

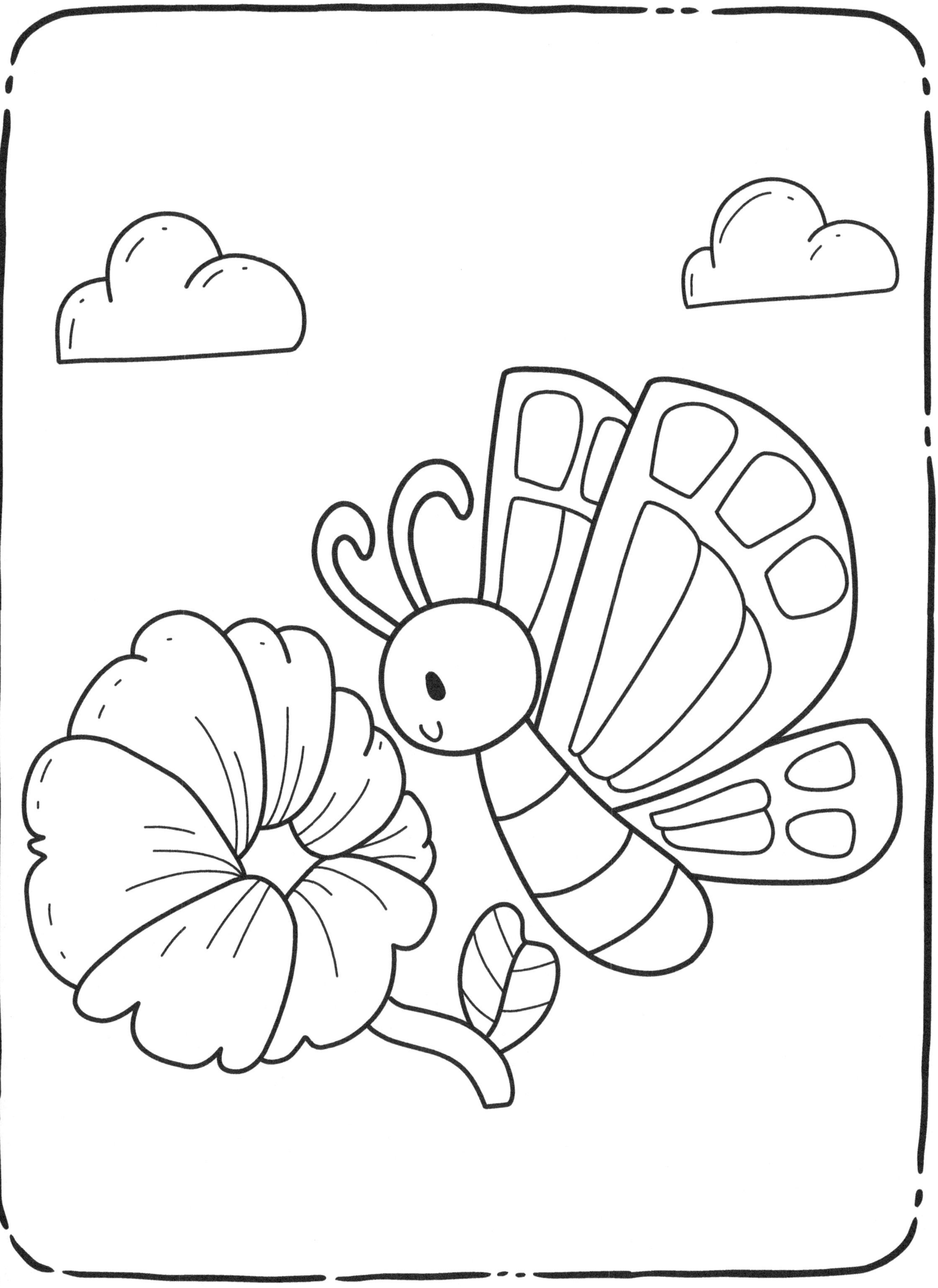

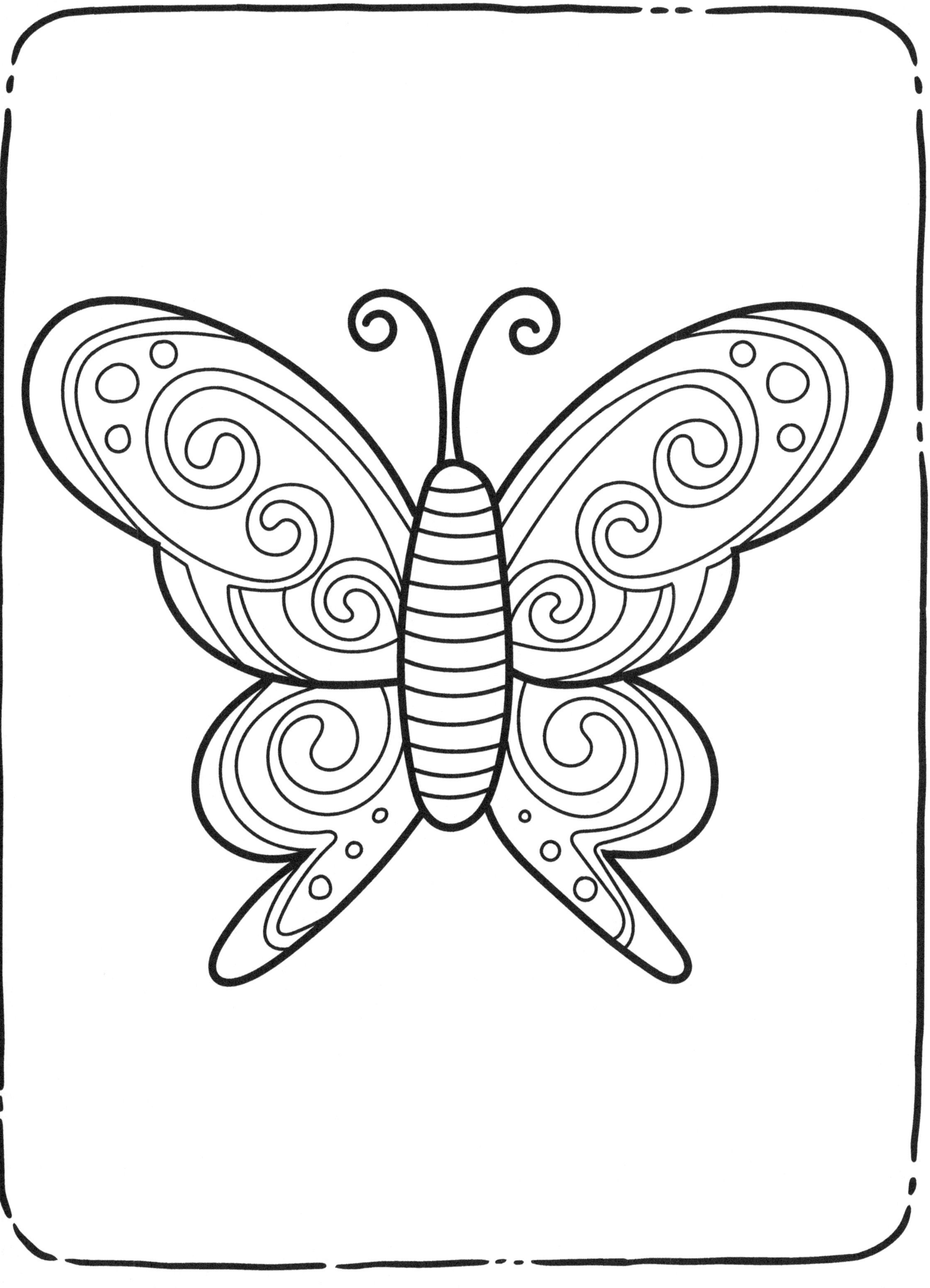

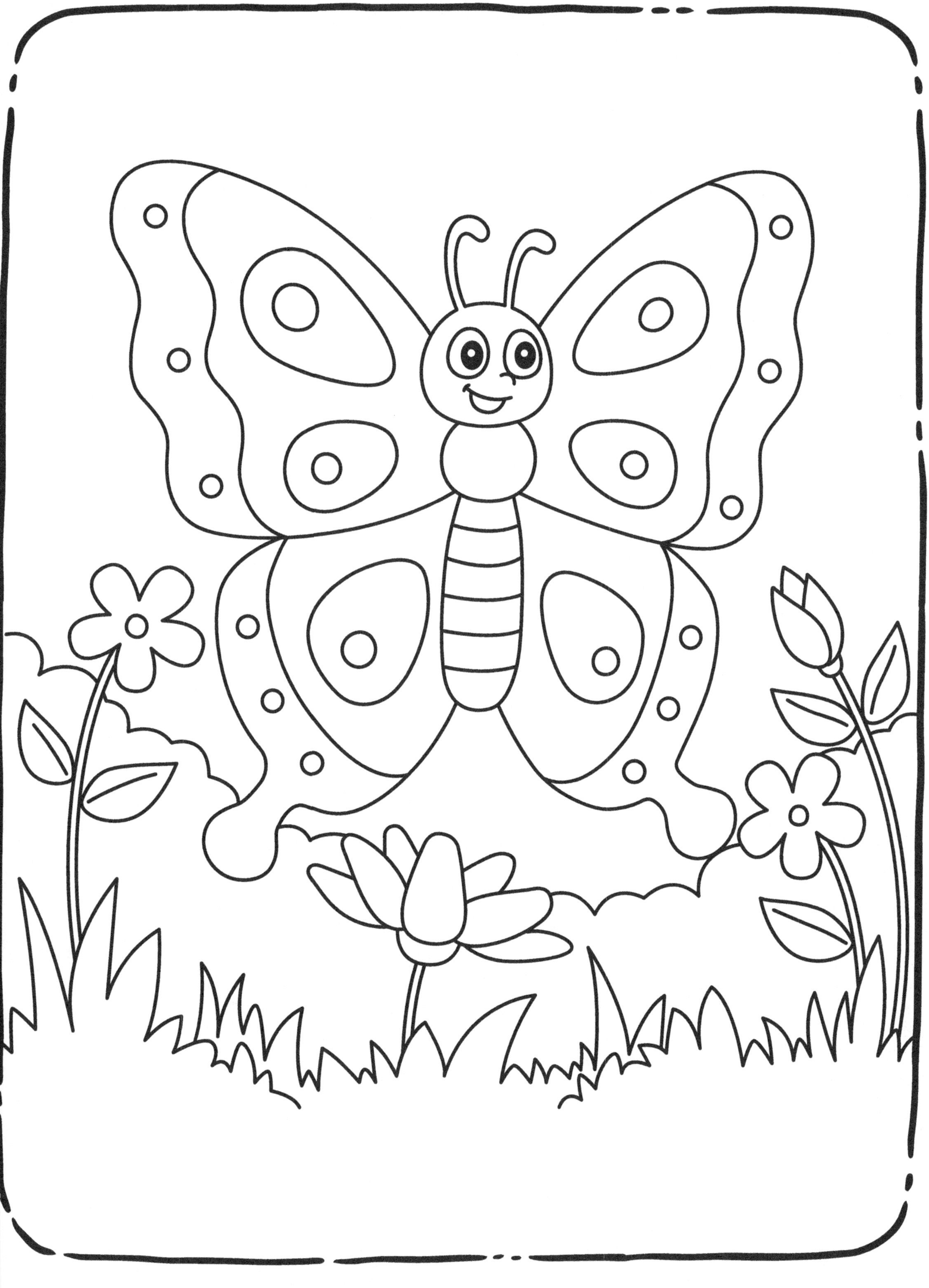

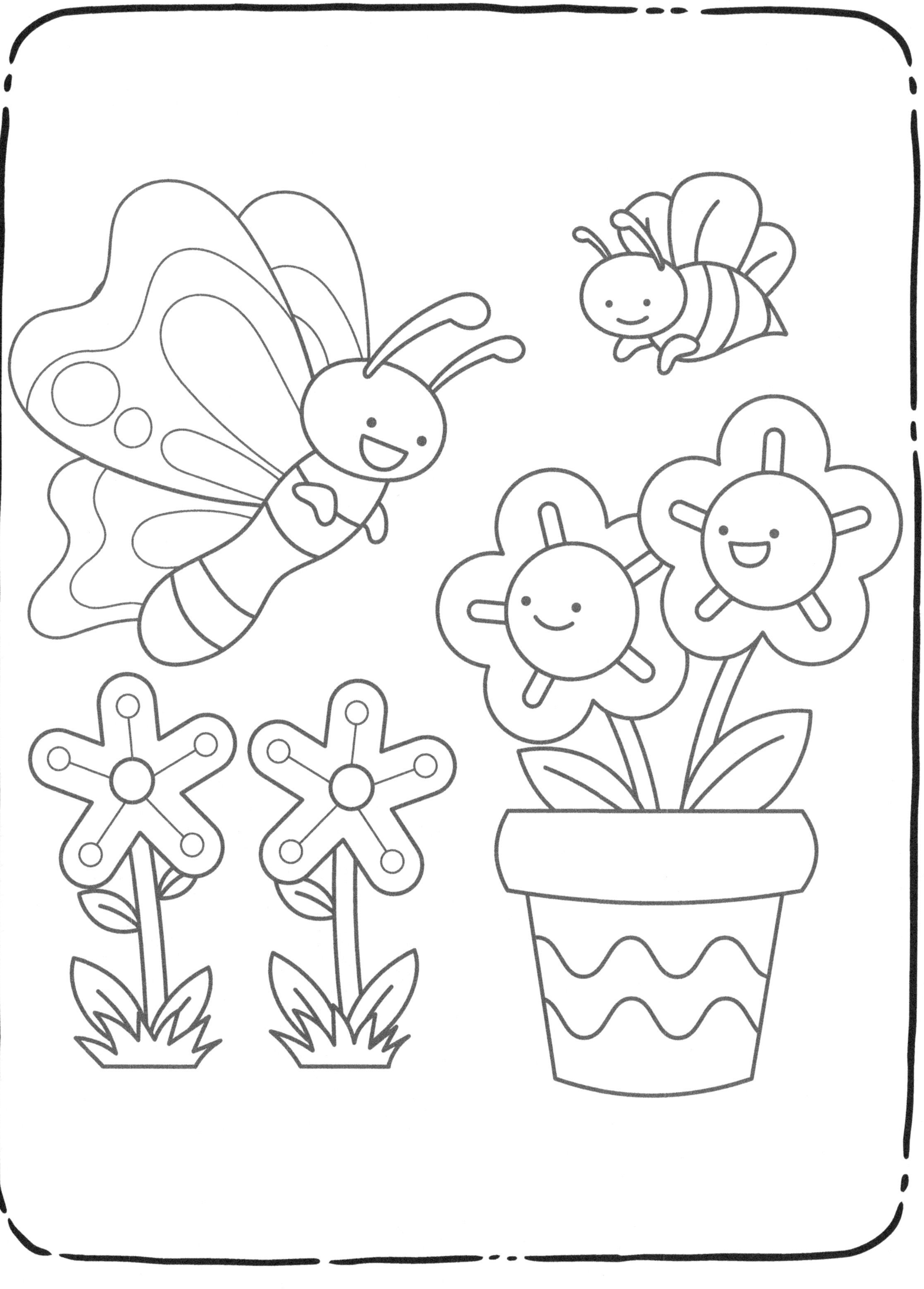

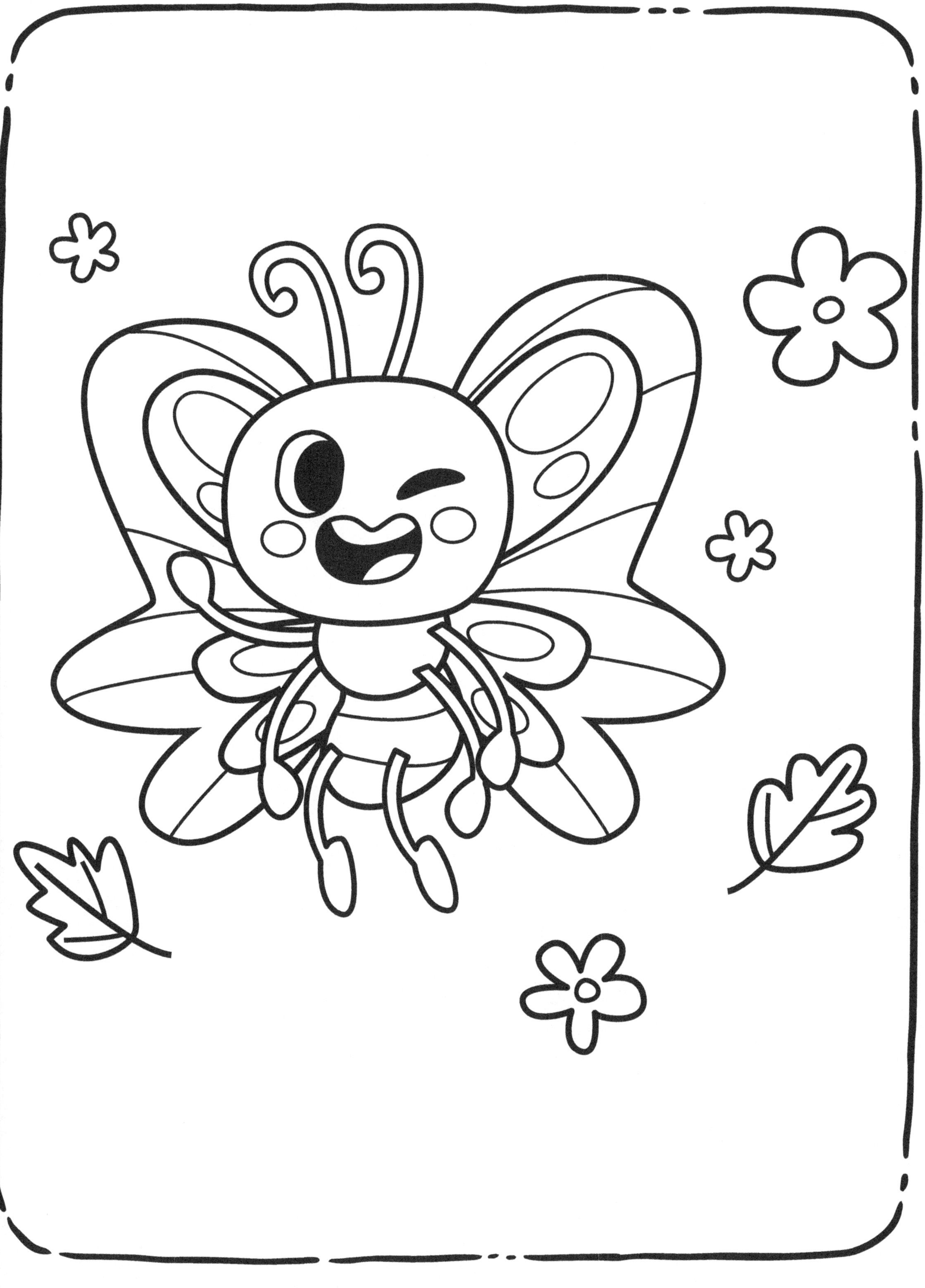

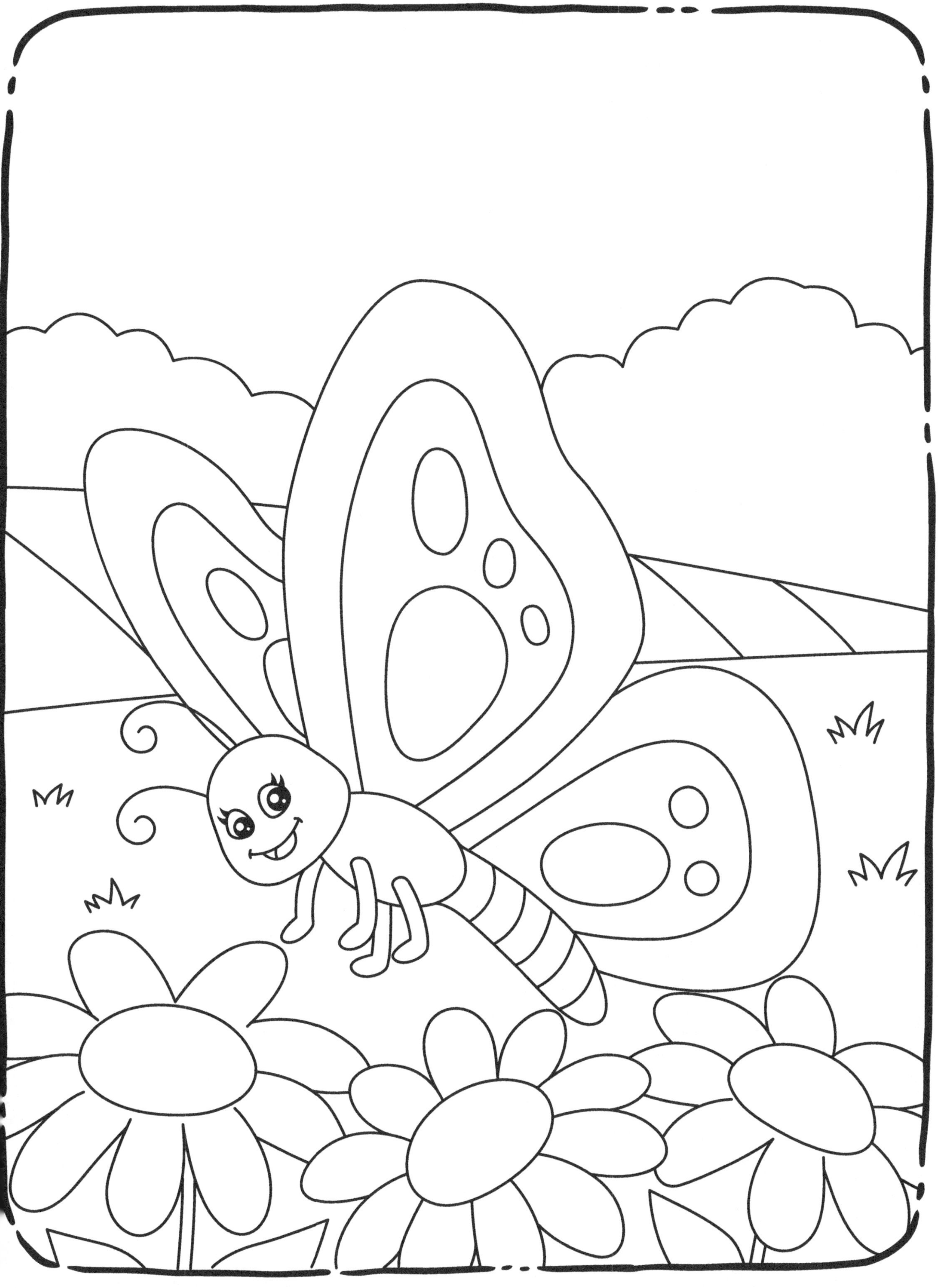

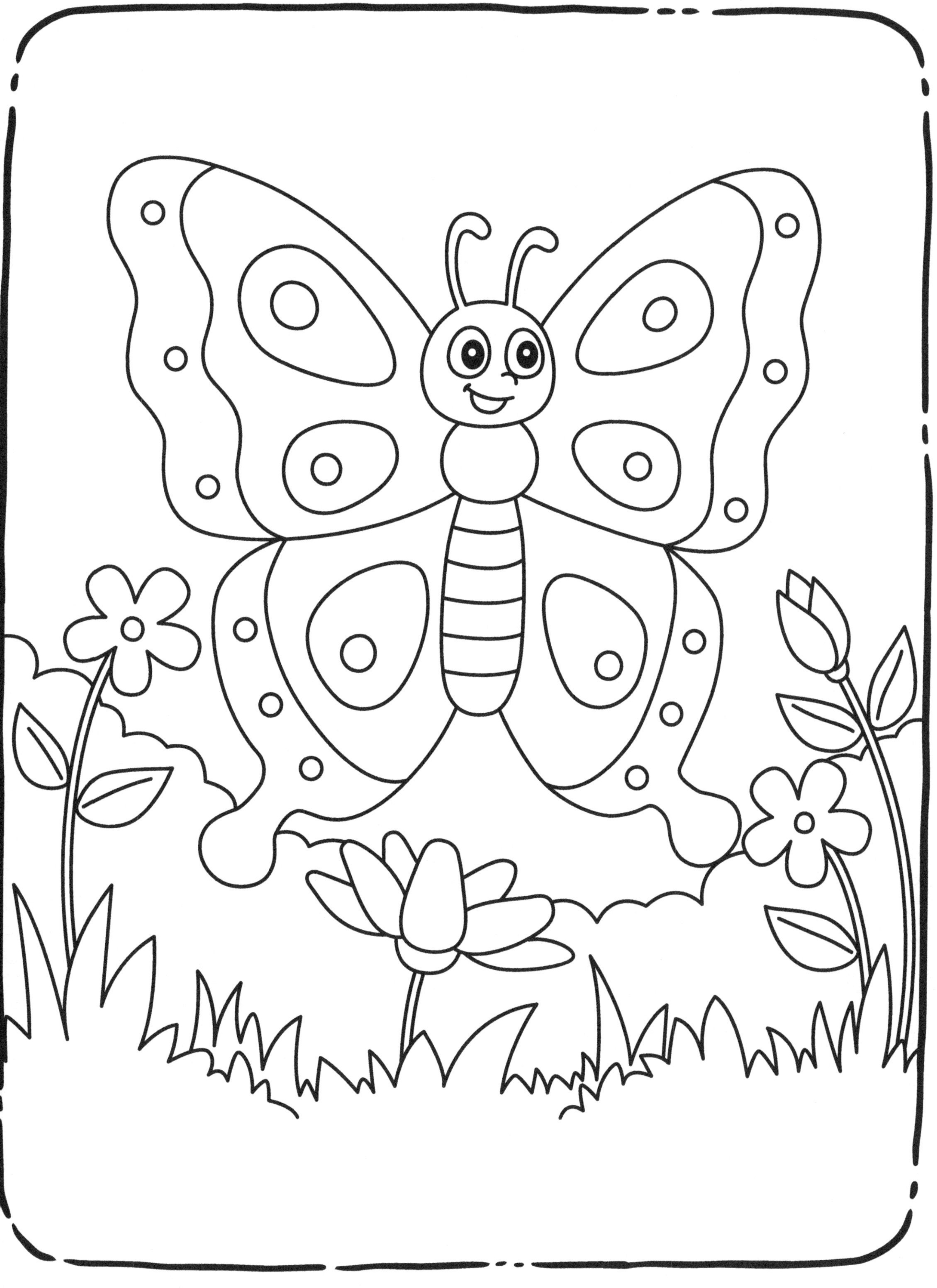

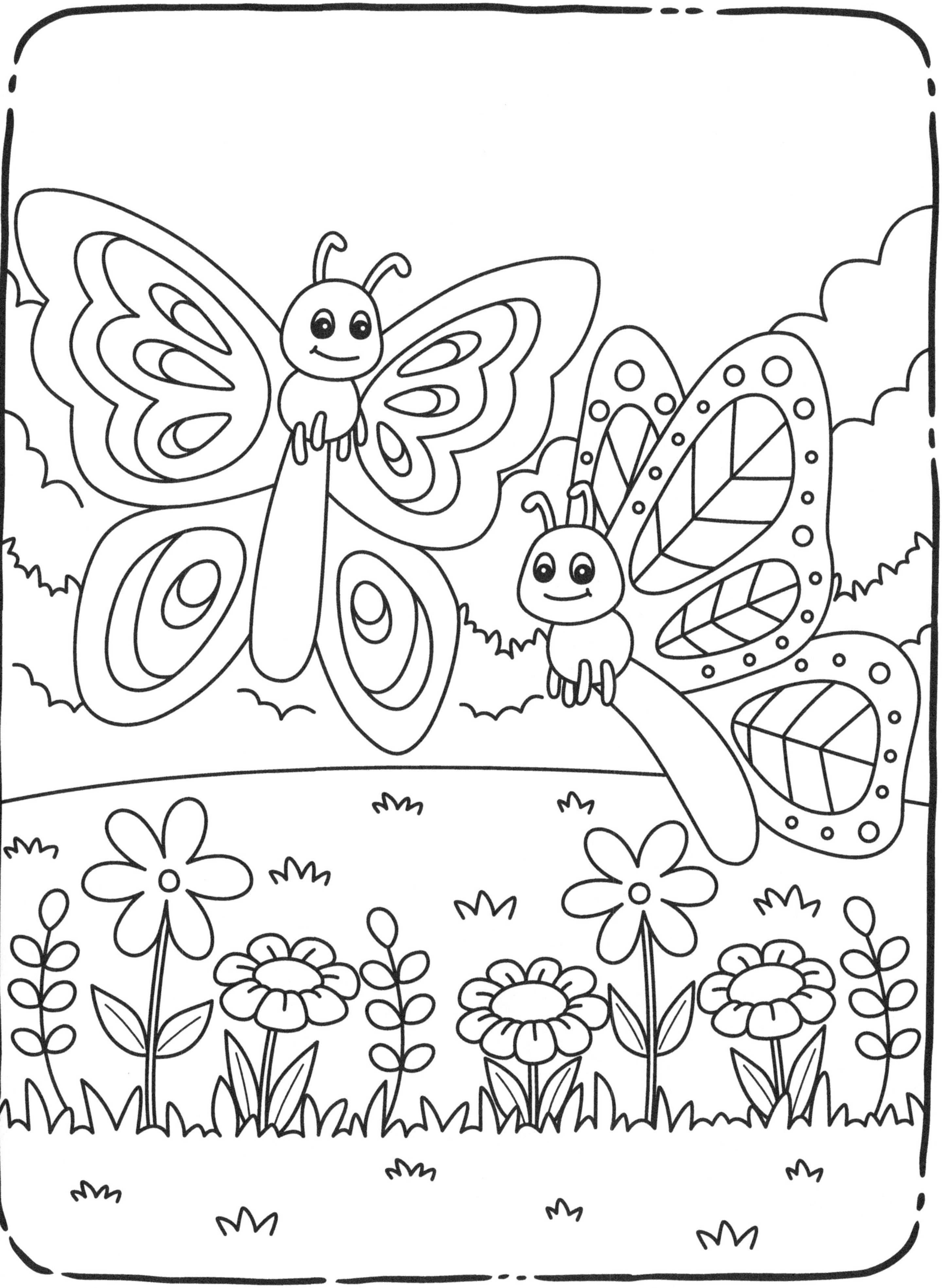

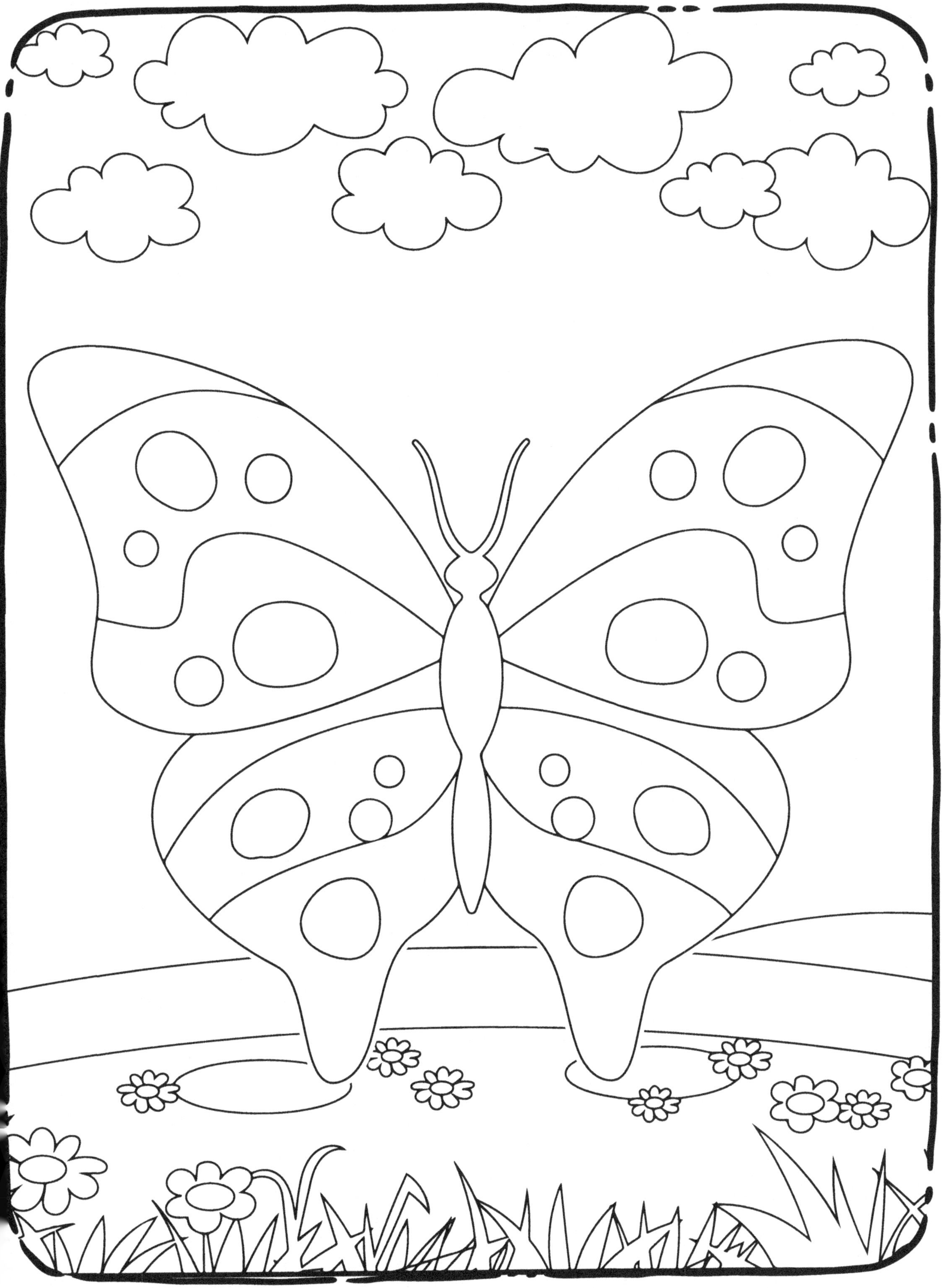

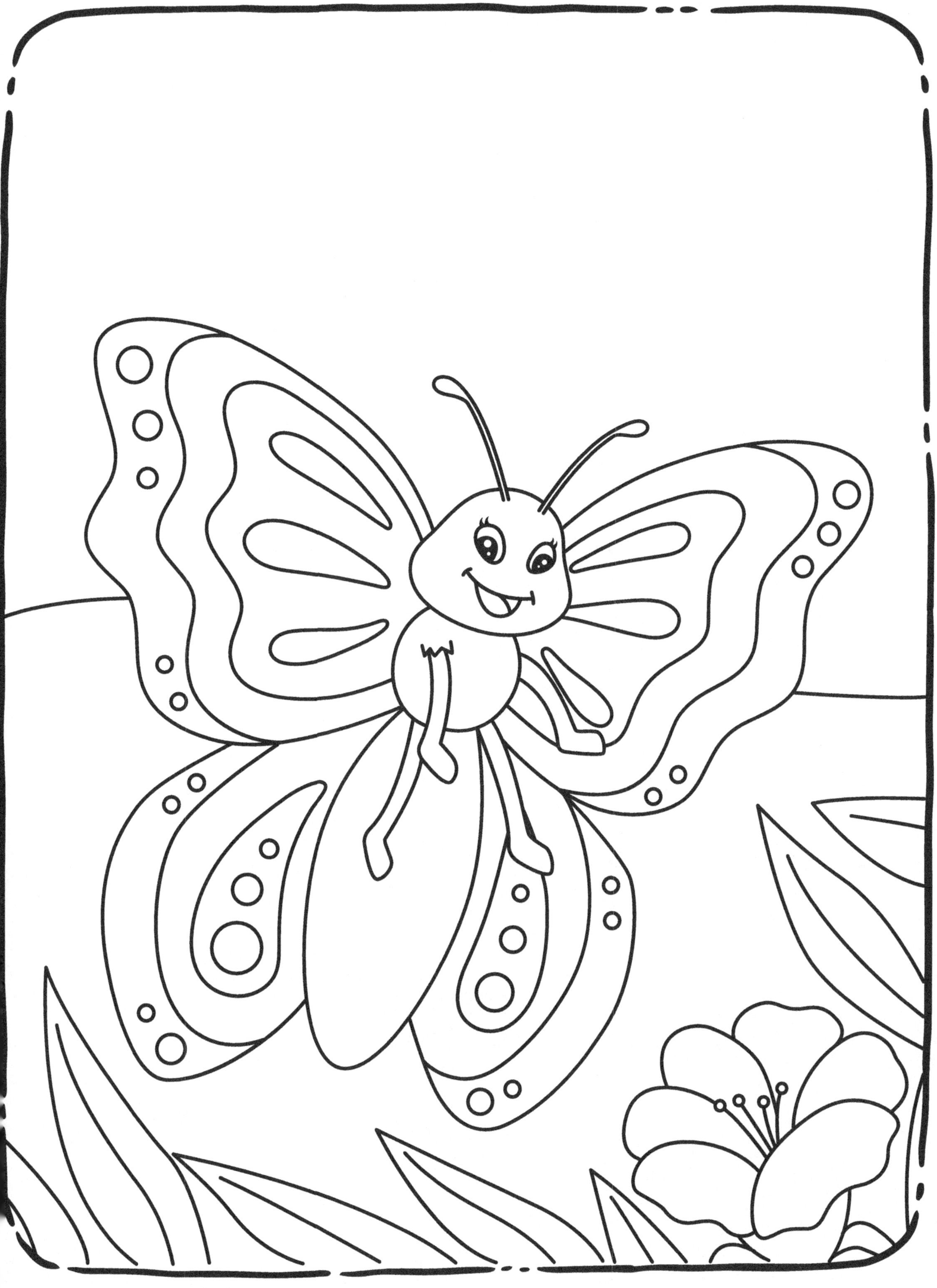

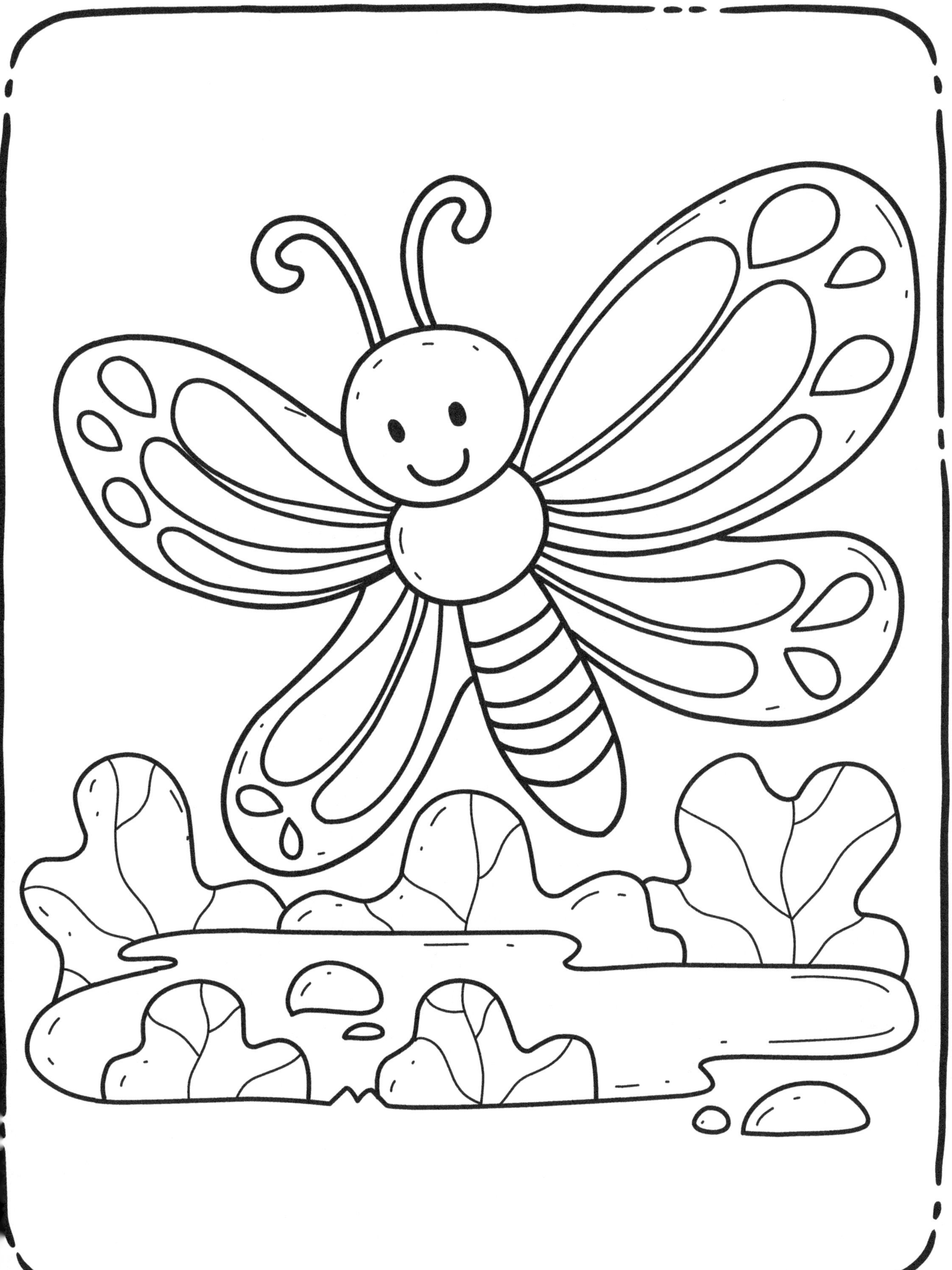

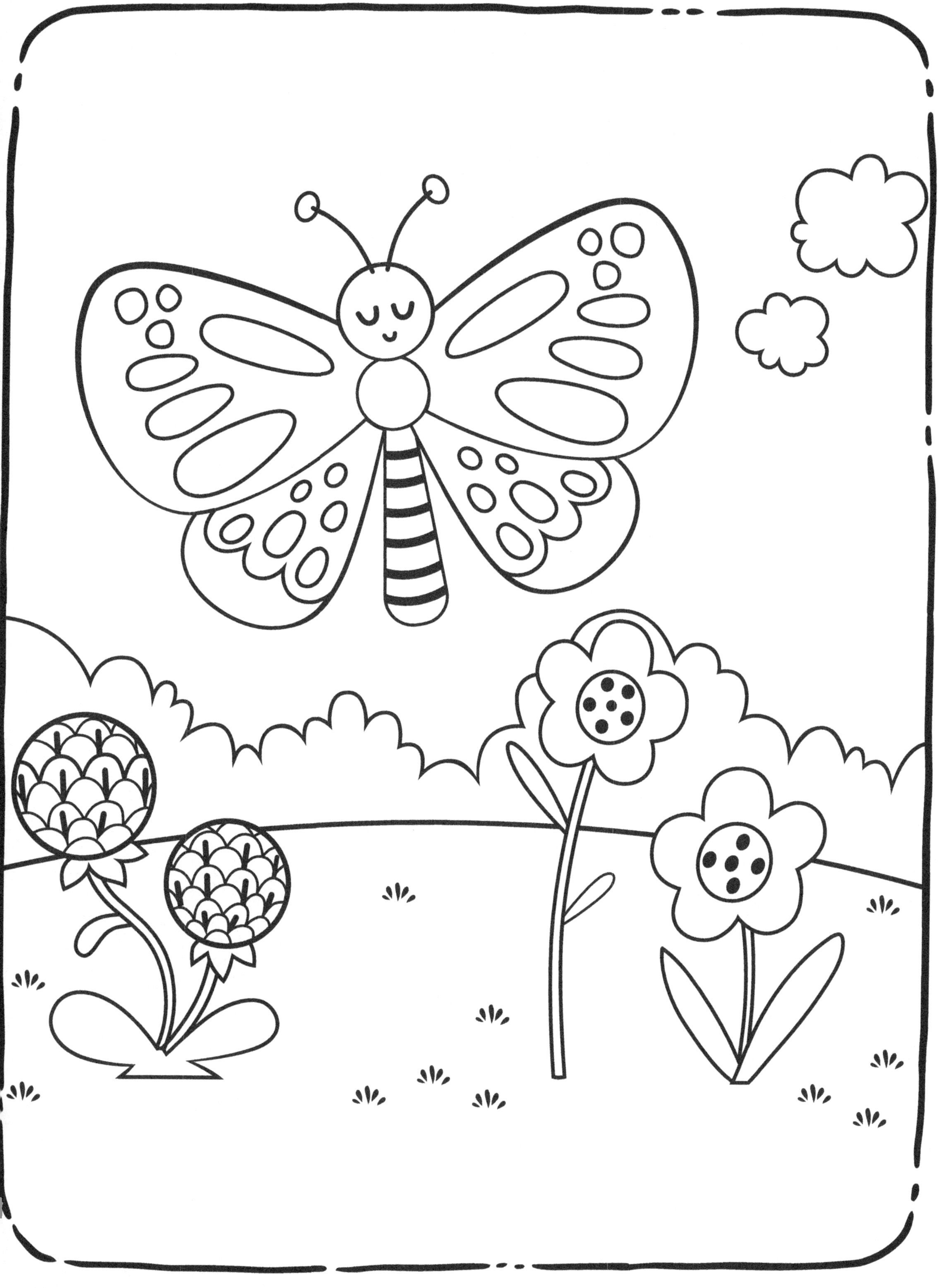

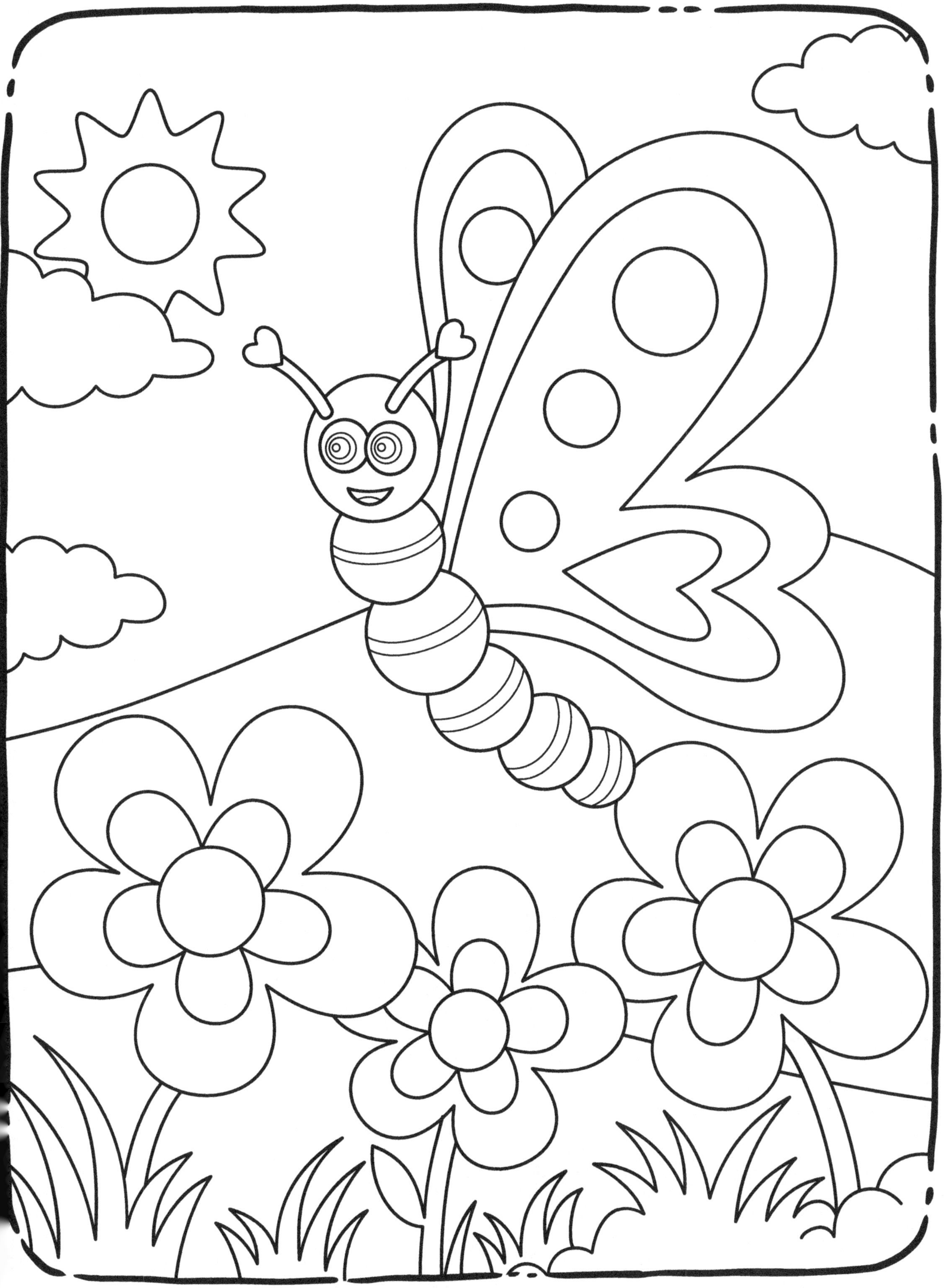

Made in the USA
Las Vegas, NV
06 November 2023

80332088R00037